BACKROADS OF AMERICA

BACKROADS OF AMERICA

DAVID COBB

CRESCENT BOOKS
NEW YORK

This 1992 edition published by CRESCENT BOOKS, distributed by Outlet Book Company, Inc., a Random House Company, 225 Park Avenue South, New York, New York 10003.

Printed and bound in Hong Kong

ISBN: 0-517-06988-1

8 7 6 5 4 3 2 1

Above: TIDAL FLATS, WASHINGTON
True to form in the country, the best vistas are off the beaten path.

Opposite: GOLD COUNTRY, CALIFORNIA
Acres of pasture and inches of shade lie under a postcard Sierra sky.

Page 1: NORTH OF ATLANTA, GEORGIA
A row of stately homes lies on the outskirts of the city.

Pages 2 - 3: THE OLD WEST CHURCH, VERMONT
Few vistas are as restful as a New England church on a clear, crisp winter evening.

Page 4: MONUMENT VALLEY, UTAH
Stretching through southern Utah and into northern Arizona, this one valley has seen everything from dinosaurs to Hollywood stars.

Page 5: TORRANCE, CALIFORNIA
Hang around Main Street in any town in America long enough, and sooner or later a parade will pass by.

Page 8: MOJAVE DESERT, CALIFORNIA
A road as straight as an arrow for as far as the eye can see may be a tempting dragstrip, but wasted gas is not such a good idea when the next fill-up is a long, hot way off.

CONTENTS

COUNTRY ROADS

BADLANDS NATIONAL PARK, SOUTH DAKOTA
A coyote glares down traffic in one of the state's most popular tourist destinations.

Then Came Bronson – Michael Parks on a Harley Sportster, crisscrossing the nation in endless search of a good script – was never much of a TV series (NBC, 1969-70), but I kept tuning in every week for the opening sequence alone. From memory, it went like this: Hot and sweaty guy, mid-forties, stressed and mortgaged, driving a monster station wagon with the air conditioner on the fritz, pulls up at a red light in Centerville, USA. In the distance the mountains shimmer in the summer smog.... Rumble rumble. Here's Parks in a skullcap (must be California), pulls up beside the wagon,

eases into neutral. He's blond, cool, laid back, the epitome of West Coast sixties' youth-chic. Forty-ish geezer leans out the window, eyes the rig, mops brow, says, "Whereya headed?" and Parks, very Brando, mumbles, "Dunno...over there" – vague gesture to the shimmering hills – "...someplace." The geezer shakes his head wryly and with the wanderlust longing of the American ages says, "Gee! Wish *I* was going." Light turns green, Parks kicks the Harley into gear, tosses a half-smile and a half-wave, and eases off into the slipstream of another weekly adventure on the open road.

Shortly after that series, and largely because of it, I became the guy on the bike, down to copying the studied Parks remoteness (the better to keep the workaday world at bay). Now of course I'm the geezer in the station wagon, increasingly trapped, for every kind of social and economic reason, at the red stoplight in the Centerville of life. But the itch is still there, the wish-*I*-was-going itch, and one day soon – who knows? Americans are the most restless people on earth and the urge to be on the road is fundamental to the national psyche.

That urge has been there since the beginning, long before there were roads to be on. It must have been there even

GATHERING BREAKFAST, FLORIDA
Grapefruits don't come much fresher than this, and if the trees are in your backyard, so much the better.

in the seventeenth and eighteenth centuries, when the first immigrants from Europe had to cling to the Atlantic seaboard, the way west barred by the Appalachians and the Apache. What wonders waited on the other side of the mountains? And at last, once over them, what wonders on the other side of the plains? "I reckon I got to light out for the Territory," said Huckleberry Finn, the quintessential American kid, and he spoke for all of us: the constant hope for change, for something better, finding it – then, as often as not, finding it not quite good enough and starting to itch all over again.

In 1790, four million Americans lived along the Atlantic shoreline, and all but five percent were rural. By 1840 the population was still 90 percent rural – and then the shift started, with vast numbers of new immigrants, population growth and increasing mobility for all. By 1920 most Americans lived in urban areas, and 85 percent will do so – forecasts the Commission on Population Growth – by the year 2000. For much of this we can thank or damn the car.

Today, with the more than 50,000 miles of engorged intestines we call the interstates intertwining across the landscape, we too easily forget the pleasures to be found on rural roads. Even more easily, with air-conditioning and cruise control and 10-speaker capability for the car stereo, we forget how hard travel used to be. People now travel for pleasure. Earlier this century, when trails were becoming roads, when only 10 percent of them were paved and all the rest were rural, when one still doubled and tripled up in stagecoach taverns and the motel was uninvented (until 1925: the Motel Inn, San Luis Obispo, California), they travelled for adventure – to "travel for travel's sake," in Robert Louis Stevenson's line. The great affair, he said, was to move.

Imagine, now, the great affair of Horatio Nelson Jackson, a 31-year-old Vermont doctor, and Sewell K. Crocker, his mechanic. In 1903, in a 20-hp Winton tourer and on a $50 bet, they made the first coast-to-coast trip by automobile. Bound for New York, they started in San Francisco. Through the isolated towns of the Rockies, Dr. Jackson recounted later, "a toot from the bulb horn ended every game of roulette and 21 as the inhabitants – sheepherders, traders, cowboys and starving Indians – crowded into the street to see the 'devil wagon.' Some of them had never heard of a car – they thought it was a small railroad engine that had somehow strayed off the tracks."

They weren't so far wrong, since Jackson and Crocker often had to drive the Winton across ravines over railroad trestles when no road bridges were available. Elsewhere, Jackson hiked 29 miles for a gas refill in Oregon; cut his own road through sagebrush in Wyoming; had to be pulled out of mud by a four-horse team in Idaho (where they also picked up a stray bulldog they named Bud, fitted him with a spare pair of goggles, and took him the rest of the way); and finally, despite nearly three weeks of delays waiting for spare parts, made it to the pavement of Park Avenue after 64 days. What better advertisement for the motorcar? Five years after that, 253 American companies were building the new horseless carriages.

That was 1908. One of the companies was Henry Ford's, and one of the new carriages that year was his Model T, which in its first year sold 5,986 copies at $850 apiece. By May, 1927, when it was finally taken off the market (last price: $360), it had sold a total of 15,007,003. The beloved Tin Lizzie may have overstayed its welcome (by 1927 it had long since been outstripped mechanically), but it can fairly be said to have ushered in the era of mass automobility on its own.

Today, when the car is under pressure from every urban planner as a street-clogging contributor to urban blight and a mobile health hazard on a par with the Scud missile, it is hard to remember how fervently the car originally was touted as the herald of a new Utopia. And to credit how well, and for how long, it fulfilled its promise. Principally, it brought better health to cities and small towns (no more horse manure, flies and related diseases), raised profits for farm communities by radically speeding up distribution, and helped lower food prices for all.

Ford, that strange combination of bigot and seer, hated the city himself ("artificial," "unnatural," "untamed and threatening... really a helpless mess") and saw the car as the means by which Americans could both escape the cities and have access to them, thus bringing urban and rural lives into

SUNRISE, WEST TENNESSEE
An ancient barn is illuminated by the early morning sun.

harmony. Technology, he believed, was "the New Messiah."

If it hasn't quite worked out that way, it's less Ford's faulty foresight than the speed with which the New Messiah set its own agenda. Increased mechanization, industrialization, centralization – steel-toed words all – have put the boots to rural harmony on a grand scale. Note the spiral: in 1929 rural farm communities accounted for 7.6 percent of the country's Gross National Product; in 1950, 4.8 percent; in 1990, 1.9 percent. In 1950, approximately 1.3 billion acres were under farm production; in 1990, 964 million acres. In the thirties there were more than six million farms in the land, many under 50 acres. Today there are some two million – a figure not quite as devastating as it looks, since the New Messiah has also brought about a great increase in productivity from any given acreage.

Not everything rural, of course, consists of the barn, the chicken-coop, the wheatfield and the range. Perhaps 25 percent of the population, or 60 million people, live outside the cities; but where in 1940 23 percent of the rural population were farmers, today only 2 percent are – and 57 percent of their net cash income comes from money made *off* the farm.

Then, in the mid-seventies something happened that ran entirely counter to form. For the first time in U.S. history rural areas started growing faster than metropolitan ones. This back-to-the-land movement had a double impetus in that it was a time of general prosperity for agriculture and simultaneously a time when many businesses, for a variety of reasons, were starting to move out of the big metropolitan areas. Between 1975 and 1980, 6.6 million people quit the

WINTER PREPARATION, PENNSYLVANIA
It may be better exercise to chop wood by hand, but when you have to lay in enough to fire the wood stove all winter, a chain saw is worth having.

EAGLE ROCK, TEXAS
Modern technology is put to use in the harvesting of
wildflower seeds.

cities and their suburbia for smaller towns and the countryside
– 3.9 million of them to southern and western states, Hawaii
and Alaska. But it did not last: the worldwide recession and
the second OPEC oil increase saw to that. Douglas Bowers,
a history specialist for the Department of Agriculture, foresees
a general stabilization in the nineties: "Rural areas are losing
population again, particularly in the midwest, but I think
we're steering a steadier course – no more that naive
confidence of the seventies when we thought farm exports
were going to go on and on forever."

Still, naive confidence (uncynical optimism, if you
prefer) is the hallmark of the American character – Scarlett's
belief that tomorrow is another day and almost certainly a
better one. The ultimate tomorrow country has always been
the American West. There, big cities are few and far between,
and society is less structured than in the rest of the country
(except Alaska). The West is the unrestricted repository of

America's mythic past, the land of outlaws, heroes, cowboys;
the land of Wild Bill Hickok and Shane, where fact and fancy
remain as improbably untramelled as the heartbreaking
landscape.

It is not a landscape for interstates; they will only take
you through it. Once on the backroads – say, to take one
random for-instance, along 18-mile Valley Drive, the dirt-
and-gravel road leading through Monument Valley, Arizona,
that was the backdrop to 101 John Wayne westerns – it takes
no time at all to fall into the rhythm of the past. The past is
all around you.

"A sharp clip-clop of iron-shod hooves deadened and
died away, and clouds of yellow dust drifted from under the
cottonwoods out over the sage..." The opening lines of Zane
Grey's *Riders of the Purple Sage* are almost 80 years old, but
in the West, where the horse still supports the cowboy and
"horse sense" may be the most highly prized of human virtues

NEAR ARCTIC VILLAGE, ALASKA
(Opposite) Some roads are more country than others. An Athabaskan Indian commutes to work in the Philip Smith Mountains.

MAN AND HIS TRUCK, HAWAII
Although pickup trucks are a common sight on backroads, few are as distinctive as the one pictured above.

(and almost totally lacking, the western theory goes, among legislators of any stripe), they carry a lot of freight even today.

The sheepman has long earned more, but the cowboy is the great American folk hero, always resourceful, forever tall in the saddle. Someone once said that the West was won by the cowboy and the schoolmarm, and who's to doubt it? As Casey Tibbs, legendary cowboy and rodeo ace, put it to me when I sought him out during a Calgary Stampede in the early sixties: "I know why y'all want to talk to me – I'm one of the last of the free men."

The cowboy as legendary frontiersman, fighting off the Comanche on one hand and Mexican banditos on the other, came into his own after the Civil War. He became a legend during the two decades of the great cattle drives from the mid-

1860s to eighties. One of the longest cattle drives was over the Goodnight-Loving Trail, from Fort Belknap, Texas, to the Pecos River, north into New Mexico and up to the railhead in Cheyenne, Wyoming: more than 1,000 miles, many of them contested with Indians, rustlers, and other dangers. No matter the fertilizer Hollywood laid on them, the Western movie had solid roots. The legend was given a tremendous kickstart by Theodore Roosevelt, who as a 25-year-old shortsighted asthmatic was sent, in 1883, to breathe the great open air on a Dakota ranch. "We knew toil and hardship and hunger and thirst," he wrote later, "but we felt the beat of hardy life in our veins, and ours was the glory of work and the joy of living." Or as he used to exclaim more colloquially: "By Godfrey but this is fun!"

SUNFLOWERS, INDIANA
A horticultural army, with faces all turned obediently
towards the sun.

It still is, but it's not quite the same. No long trail drives (the tractor-trailers take care of that); no three-day rides to reach the cattle for roundup (they drive there now, trucking their horses behind them); fewer than half the cowboy complement of a century ago (down from some 40,000 in the 1880s). "And many of the new ones are women," says Alex Dees, a 52-year-old cattleman in Winterhaven, California, on the Arizona border. "It's as tough a business as ever it was – but at least we get driven to the cattle today. We can do three times the work we did before in half the time. No pickups or ATVs to help us when I started out back in the fifties. And in some of the big spreads in Texas they use helicopters too."

One thing stays the same: the cowboy's low wages. At the low end it's about $450 a month, at the high, $1,200.

This includes room and (usually) a vehicle for one's own use; but no food apart from the occasional slab of beef.

"So it's very difficult to find good labor," says Tom Rolston, a ranch broker in Phoenix. "You want intelligent people who've been raised round livestock, but they know they can do more with their lives than punch cattle. Then you find one, and all he wants to do is ride horses because that's the romantic thing, what the wide open spaces are about. But there's much more to it than that – there's fixing fences today, and changing the oil in the pickup, and Western movies have never shown that."

Today's youth is more college-oriented: the heroes are Michael Jordan and André Agassi, who have seven or eight

hundred hp waiting for them in the carport; not Gene Autry and Roy Rogers. Very few dream of working their way up to buy a ranch one day.

And yet. The reality of the West may be changing, and good help may continue to be hard to find there, but the image of the range, so deeply imbedded, dies hard, indeed will probably never die at all. Something of it is stamped forever in the American consciousness, at the base of every backroad of the mind. It triggers the itch that Huck Finn scratched when he felt he had to light out for the Territory; the same itch that drove Bronson every week across America on his Harley, and every viewer with him; the endless itch towards innocence and discovery.

Somewhere... down the next few country roads... over the next range of hills... there will be something uncluttered and closer to nature: something better. Always.

VALLEY DRIVE, ARIZONA
(Opposite) Although there are no sidewalks and no lights, traffic still has to stop for the Monument Valley version of pedestrians – a herd of Navajo sheep and goats.

DANIEL BOONE NATIONAL FOREST, KENTUCKY
Early morning mist drops a muted veil over the fall colors along the Red River Gorge.

FOOTHILLS, ROCKY MOUNTAINS, MONTANA
Big Sky country takes on a decidedly threatening tone as
an alpine storm builds from the west.

SWEET GRASS HILLS, MONTANA
(Previous pages) The early morning light lends a purplish
cast to the Sweet Grass Hills.

UPSTATE NEW YORK
The rising of the sun is a familiar sight to most farmers.

SUPPERTIME ON THE RANGE
Beans, bacon, biscuits and coffee thick enough to tar the
road. In a scene that has changed little in over 100 years,
cowboys Ken Spaan and Bill Rivale dine at sunset.

SANTA YNEZ, CALIFORNIA
In the coastal mountains north of Los Angeles, the image
of the lonesome cowboy sometimes suffers from a lack of
elbow room.

PENNY'S LUNCH, MAINE
Featuring some of the best food going, roadside takeouts
are a popular sight on country roads.

CALIFORNIA DESERT
A gas station and adjoining café provide a welcome oasis
in the California desert.

TULIP FIELD, LA CONNER, WASHINGTON
They may be the most fragrant and most attractive crop
around, but one wonders if these harvesters would ever
send tulips to their sweethearts.

MUSTARD FIELD, TENNESSEE
A vivid mustard field stands in full bloom at high noon.

SUGAR CABIN, READING, VERMONT
In the Vermont mountains, the first snow is usually on
the ground to stay weeks before the last leaves fall.

PUMPKIN PATCH, NEW HAMPSHIRE
They may not win any ribbons at the fall fair, but at least
these pumpkins are safe from the crows.

MOJAVE DESERT
A stark roadside tree offers scant shade in southern
California.

STEAMBOAT SPRINGS, COLORADO
Twilight surrounds a winter traveller's last stop of the day.

LOBSTER BUOYS, MAINE
Like a rancher's cattle brand, lobster fishermen color-code
their trap markers.

LIVERY STABLE, DAMELE RANCH, NEVADA
The rancher's version of a toolbox comes complete with
anvil and cats.

SMOKY MOUNTAINS, TENNESSEE
(Following pages) The view from this country road shows
why Cherokee Indians, the orginal residents of the area,
called it Shaconage – "Place of Blue Smoke."

CHATTAHOOCHEE NATIONAL FOREST, GEORGIA
A rookie angler and his baiter look for a keeper north of
Atlanta.

SUNSET, OREGON
A sunset provides just enough time to get the fish stories
straight before heading home.

NORTH CONWAY, NEW HAMPSHIRE
What country road would be complete without a covered
bridge? And if you want to go from Conway to Intervale,
North Conway will oblige, unless you drive a truck.

YELLOWSTONE NATIONAL PARK, WYOMING
Established in 1872, Yellowstone is America's most
popular national park, attracting over two million visitors
a year. On the day above, a lone skier has the place to
himself.

HARDY COUNTY, WEST VIRGINIA
Both buildings wouldn't add up to one square corner, but
then the land isn't exactly level either.

SAGUARO NATIONAL MONUMENT, ARIZONA
A prime specimen of an endangered symbol of the
American southwest. Because of pollution, urban sprawl
and its status as a tempting target for some gun owners,
the Giant Saguaro cactus had all but disappeared. The
National Parks Service has now established two protected
areas near Tucson to preserve the rare desert giant.

DUST STORM, KANSAS
As hazardous to driving as any blizzard and able to strip
the paint off a car, a farmer's nightmare blows up out of
nowhere.

WIND CAVE NATIONAL PARK, SOUTH DAKOTA
According to more than one ballad of the Old West, the
outlaw ended up swinging from a cottonwood tree, much
like this one in South Dakota.

SAN JUAN MOUNTAINS, COLORADO
Stretching from southwest Colorado almost to Sante Fe,
New Mexico, the San Juan Mountains provide the source
for one of America's great rivers, the Rio Grande.

WHITE-TAILED DEER, WYOMING
In the country, wildlife often isn't much farther than the side of the road.

MIDDLEBURY, VERMONT
A fall ritual, the maple sap is collected fresh from the tree and then transferred to the horse-drawn tank.

SQUASH WASHING, FLORIDA
In Florida City, between Everglades National Park and Miami, Cornelius and Sons Produce Inc. prepares the day's harvest for market.

Is This Heaven?
Close, it's Iowa.

SADDLE ROAD, HAWAII
Saddle Road runs along the western slope of Mauna Kea,
the island's, and the state's, highest point.

MILE 247, TEXAS
(Opposite) Dusk on the highway with a slow shutter speed.
Away from city lights the moon takes on an extra glow.

TALIMENA DRIVE, ARKANSAS
A slow, winding road in the South provides the perfect
autumn drive in the country.

MORNING ROUNDS, ILLINOIS
In a scene repeated in countless rural communities across
America, the local commuter service heads out to pick up
its charges.

STONE LAGOON, OREGON
This quintessential little red schoolhouse is now a
museum catering to the bargain-hunting traveller.

LETTUCE HARVEST, WASHINGTON
Come rain or shine, the lettuce must be harvested.

HARVEST, NORTH DAKOTA
A good crop can mean plenty of overtime, but with a view
like the one at left it's hard to mind.

NEAR DEARBORN, MONTANA
Not all backroads lead to a specific destination. Some
just fade into the fields.

ORFORD, NEW HAMPSHIRE
For some, the last turn up the driveway is another quarter
mile of picture-perfect fences and overhanging trees.

CANOLA FIELDS, NORTH DAKOTA
(Opposite) The latest discovery in healthy eating makes a pretty picture before packaging.

NAVAJO HOGAN, ARIZONA
An eight-sided log and mud Navajo *hogan*, or lodge, is as unique and spectacular as any architecture in the world.

TOBACCO FARM, NEW YORK
It pays to advertise, especially if you have a stake in the business.

HUDSON RIVER VALLEY, NEW YORK
No additives, no preservatives, and no charge for field dirt still attached.

NEAR BOULDER, COLORADO
"You can't miss it – red barn, white house, *big* backyard."

OREGON
If the temperature drops low enough, even the
ever-present Pacific coast fog freezes.

EAST FORK OF THE SALMON RIVER, IDAHO
Two icons of the Old West in central Idaho – lonesome hills
and sagebrush.

EAST ORANGE, VERMONT
A perfect place for a fall walk, with crackling leaves and a
gravel road underfoot.

BELL RANCH ROUNDUP, NEW MEXICO
For workers in the country, the first meal of the day is
usually long before sunrise.

NAVAJO LAND, ARIZONA
Modern-day totems offer a welcome change from the
all-too-prolific highway billboard.

Locust Creek, West Virginia
The older the covered bridge, the tighter the squeeze for modern motorized traffic. Bicycles, however, have never been a problem.

STOWE, VERMONT
A skier's dream – clear skies, lots of snow and a working
fireplace at the end of the trail.

FAIRBURY, NEBRASKA
The wind-driven water pump is almost a symbol of the prairie.

NEAR HELIX, OREGON
Most country roads follow the contours of the land underneath, and in some cases a quiet drive can become a roller coaster ride worthy of any amusement park.

CATTLE DRIVE, IDAHO
Motorists beware: cattle in southeast Idaho pay little
attention to the yellow line.

HIGH COUNTRY, MONTANA
On a country road, there's usually great scenery over the next hill.

SHENANDOAH VALLEY, VIRGINIA
Amish farmers ride their horses and buggies along a
backroad in the Shenandoah Valley.

Near Burlington, Vermont
The white clapboard house and white three-rail fence are a prime example of traditional New England architecture.

LAKE MICHIGAN
A group of children indulge in one of summer's greatest
pleasures.

ADIRONDACKS, NEW YORK
The Mountain Pond Road typifies the kind of roadside
scenery to be found, particularly in the fall, in
northeastern New York.

RUNNING HORSES, COLORADO
The foothills of the Rockies offer a dramatic backdrop to a
herd of running horses.

DAIRY CATTLE, WASHINGTON
A passerby earns a skeptical look from a grazing cow.

COUNTRY STORE, GEORGIA
(Following page) Herman Johnson, proprietor, stands in
front of his store in Gwinnett County.

MAIN STREET

FOOTBALL GAME, GEORGIA
Cheerleaders raise the spirits of the crowd at a college football game.

Small town. Short of the scatological or profane, what other two words pack more potent emotional freight? Small-town person, small-town values: depending on how you say them they can be profoundly sentimental, crushingly condescending, and sometimes a mix of both. Even if we've never lived in one, we know exactly what we mean by the descriptives, and (especially if we've never lived in one) the physical image has been burned into our minds by a thousand movies and books and television shows. The old but neatly painted houses... the office of the weekly *Times*... the corner store... the five-and-

dime... Harry's soda fountain... the movie theater... the two-wicket bank... the pool hall... the furniture store... the town seats on the green under the chestnut trees... and at night under the stars an absolute quietness broken only by the mournful call of a loon on a nearby lake.

The idea of the small town was perfected in New England – "the first American section," in author Bernard De Voto's phrase, "to be finished." But wherever we place it in our mind's eye there's no denying its power. Not long ago a national magazine polled more than a thousand people on where they'd like to buy a new home: 94 percent voted for rural areas and small towns, anywhere well away from big cities. Increasingly cities are associated with muggings and triple-locked doors, lousy air, doubtful water, stress and the rat race; places where one lives only because one has to.

Small towns obviously must be the reverse: places where seldom is heard a discouraging word and the skies are unpolluted all day. Sure, education opportunities may be fewer, but nobody starts learning much before university anyway; incomes may be lower, but so's the cost of living; and on those rare occasions when the body cries out for a smack of stress and sin, if only to remind it what they mean – well, it can head for the nearest interstate. The big city is never that far away.

According to this scenario small-town life is the best of all possible American worlds. The hold it exerts, often by those who don't live it, has not changed much in the century since Mark Twain, on a speaking tour of India, remarked pensively that "all the me in me is in a little Missouri village half-way round the world." The village was Hannibal, on the banks of the Mississippi, where Twain grew up with fewer than a thousand other inhabitants in the 1840s and fifties.

Nobody pitched the social and moral virtues of small-town life with more fervor than Booth Tarkington in *The Gentleman from Indiana* (1899). The gent is John Harkless, who for the sake of his career finds himself in New York, where he becomes a newspaper editor. The rat race appals him: "The cruel competition, the thousands fighting for places... the cold faces on the streets... I wanted to get out of it." So he does, back to Plattville, Indiana: "I always had a dim sort of feeling that people out in these parts knew more – had more *sense* and were less artificial, I mean – and were kinder,

OGUNQUIT, MAINE
As in most seaside towns, Main Street can be found along the water.

FAIRBANKS, ALASKA
If the accommodations are a little cramped and the view a
little limited, one just makes the hole bigger.

and tried less to be somebody else, than almost any other people anywhere." And there, after many trials and tribulations, and getting most unkindly beaten half to death by a bunch of hooded trash known as the Whitecaps (forerunners of the Ku Klux Klan twenty years later), Harkless delivers a paean to the Plattville townsfolk, ending: "This is the place for the man who likes to live... and where they have the old-fashioned way of saying 'Home.'"

A century later the same idea remains: that small-town life embodies all that's best in American life, a microcosm of unity and decency. The idea has not had it all its own way by any means. Twenty years after Tarkington's book came out, the concept was as badly mugged as Harkless by the Whitecaps. The muggers were Sherwood Anderson in *Winesburg, Ohio*

(1919) and Sinclair Lewis in *Main Street* (1920), and they delivered two of the most devastating body blows small-town life has ever received. The lifestyle itself – the comforting sense of unity – was damned for stifling individuality; small-town people were mercilessly satirized as gossipy, small-minded and smug.

The attacks were ferocious, enormously successful in their time, and remain mainstays of twentieth-century American literature courses. But a funny thing happened on the way to the grave: in the fullness of time both authors recanted. In 1940, the year before he died, Anderson wrote: "The big world outside now is so filled with confusion, it seems to me that our only hope, in the present muddle, is to try thinking small." And in later life, too, Lewis acknowledged

MIDDLEBURY, VERMONT
A postcard version of America's Main Street, complete
with a pristine church at one end.

that part of him was forever indebted to Sauk Centre, Minnesota (the model for *Main Street*'s Gopher Prairie). Sauk Centre knows it's somehow forever indebted to Lewis, too, even in reverse: at the town's only stoplight, Sinclair Lewis Avenue bisects what it now proudly calls "The Original Main Street."

Perhaps their recanting had its roots, despite all, in a very American optimism. Once, thank heaven, free at last of the intense middlingness of small-town life, the boil lanced by lampooning the life to a fare-thee-well, they thought again and weighed what they had gained, what they had lost.

The greatest visual chronicler of that life was Norman Rockwell, who as a child sketched an event from the end of the Spanish-American War and lived to portray man's first

step on the moon. Rockwell, who died in 1978, was himself a living embodiment of the continuity of the small-town life he created so memorably for the old *Saturday Evening Post* from the thirties through the fifties. And as such he laid himself open to attacks every bit as corrosive as those visited by Anderson and Lewis on their small towns.

The assaults came mainly from big-city critics, galleries and artists, most of whom doubtless never forgave him for the unforgivable amount of money he made. Or for his subject matter. Rockwell, who never took himself too seriously, was always careful to call himself an illustrator rather than an artist – "and country people do fit my kind of picture better than city people," he said.

The fashionable put-down has always been that

Rockwell portrayed a romanticized small-town America "that never existed." On a basic level this is ludicrous, because after an unhappy spell in New York suburbia Rockwell spent his creative life in small towns (and his most productive years in Arlington, Vermont: current pop. 2,000). His meticulous observation and attention to detail were bywords. They had to be: every illustration had to pass the scrutiny of the *Post*'s four million readers, who pounced on the slightest error or anachronism.

Certainly he shunned the unpleasant, the sordid, the tragic; he avoided depression and even (much more amazing) the Depression. He was not a Daumier or a Goya – he would have been quick to point out they were artists. What he did create, within his limits, were utterly recognizable small-town characters in a perfectly realized small-town world. Being young, falling in love, growing old; Mom and Dad and the kids; the doctor, the banker, the returning soldier, the town character; the card game, the soda fountain – these were the universal characters and timeless themes which were his forte. Someone was once asked what James Stewart was like in person. "He's a very Norman Rockwell kind of a guy," was the reply, a tribute to both actor and illustrator.

The city slickers who say it was a world that never was merely revealed (and still reveal) the depth of their ignorance of small towns. Rockwell knew where they were coming from, anyway. As he once observed of the spare, self-contained, intensely individualistic Vermonters of Arlington: "None of that sham

'I am *so* glad to know you!' accompanied by radiant smiles. They shook my hand, said 'How do' and waited to see how I would turn out. Not hostile, but reserved, with a dignity and personal integrity which are rare in suburbia, where you are familiar with someone before you know him."

Rockwell would have been right at home in New Harmony, the remarkable little Indiana town where the population has stayed between 800 and 900 for more than 150 years and is not likely to change, since it's hemmed in by hills on two sides and the Wabash River on the other two, for the next 150.

This alone would hardly make New Harmony remarkable. What does, for a town this size, is its remarkable series of firsts, which make it a kind of paragon for small towns everywhere. America's first school for infants (an advanced form of day care, in 1826). First free educational school. First trade school. First scientific archaeological digs. First organized acting school. And one of the first libraries in

MINNEAPOLIS, MINNESOTA
It's forty below and the next time this bicycle will be ridden is likely to be during spring thaw. Given all this, the lock seems redundant.

the U.S. and certainly the oldest (built in 1838) in Indiana.

It is also the first place to have used, between 1815 and 1825, prefab construction for housing, some of which still exists in the town. This was the brainchild of New Harmony's founder, a Lutheran pastor named George Rapp. Father Rapp believed in the Second Coming of Christ in Jerusalem, and to raise the wherewithal to get there, organized his followers into an extremely profitable unit. So successful were they that 10 years later the Harmonists were making money hand over fist, selling silk and woollen goods, citrus fruits and furniture to 22 states and 10 foreign countries. It was Rapp's Utopia: the money made was to the common cause; property was held communally; and celibacy was the strict order of the day and night.

Alas, there is always a worm in the garden of Eden, even in Indiana, and even in a place called New Harmony. Bickering started (they were making a lot of money but maybe not enough), and enforced celibacy ensured a constant decline in numbers. In 1824 the Harmonists bailed out for Pennsylvania (the last one dying, still waiting for the Second Coming, in 1905) and Father Rapp sold the settlement to Robert Owen.

Owen, a British social reformer, was another remarkable man. He set about forming his own Utopia, this one based on no religion at all but common sense, and aimed at setting up the most enlightened society that scientists and educators could devise. It was under his leadership and his son's that most of New Harmony's firsts occurred. The Owen concept of communal living – no paid workers, but a lot of unpaid

CHRISTMAS, COLORADO
In preparation for Christmas, the lamp-posts are garlanded with wreaths.

thought – attracted a lot of freeloaders and failed to build a solid middle class. The result was no more lastingly successful for Owen than it had been for Father Rapp, and by 1830 New Harmony's second Utopian experiment had bitten the dust.

And today? Some would say that New Harmony has developed into the Utopia of small towns – a perfect place to live now that its days of impractical schemes for social betterment are in the past. "There's no new building here because there's no spare land to build on," says Julie Rutherford, New Harmony's town promotion coordinator. "So it's a very pretty town, not much built after 1910. Nobody locks their cars or their doors at night. You say Hi, how are you? and you wait for the reply. At Wilson Furniture on Main Street five men sit in the window drinking coffee, watching people walk by, every day of their lives... No hustle and bustle. It's an ideal life."

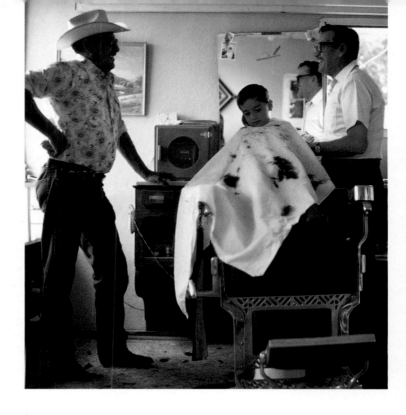

BARBERSHOP, NEW MEXICO
A young boy undergoes his first
haircut in this timeless scene.

CATAWBA, NORTH CAROLINA
(Opposite) A general store constitutes one-stop shopping
for the community in and around town, and in Catawba
everybody goes to Murray & Minges, who will sell you
anything from a hat to a kosher dill.

Mrs. Rutherford was born close to New Harmony and says she may soon move into the town itself. "In the first half of the year 15 people have died here. So there are a few places to buy, quite unusual. People come here, they tend to stay, it's like travelling back into time."

It's probably because of the town's enduring small-town virtues that, in 1991, Columbia Pictures went to New Harmony to shoot a key part of *A League of Their Own*. It stars Geena Davis, Tom Hanks and Madonna, and it's about women baseball players who formed their own league during the Second World War. All Columbia had to do was take down a few power lines, street lamps and the odd anachronistic air conditioner. New Harmony did the rest.

Plainly not your everyday small town. And the more you travel off the beaten track the more you find how different each town is. A lot of the ingredients may be the same north and south, east and west, but for a lasting idea of what keeps so much of America healthy, towns should always be sampled at source. Blasting along interstates, with the occasional turnoff for gas and a spot of local color, is not the way to do it. Superhighways can be even more impersonal than the view from a jet at 25,000 feet on a clear day.

The backroads connecting all our Main Streets are the way to go if you are in search of a sense of place. Where else will you find such diversity, or so many world capitals without capital pretensions? The world capital of cotton, say, or tobacco, or corn, or catfish, or peaches, or perogies? Or, say again, of old-time bartering (Canton, Texas, where 5,000 dealers spread across more than a hundred acres sell and barter over a three-day weekend once a month)? Or, breathe gently, of garlic (Gilroy, California, which on the last full weekend in every July attracts upwards of 140,000 people to sample such exceptional byproducts of the stinking rose as garlic ice cream, washed down with a flagon or two of garlic wine)?

Last word to Thorstein Veblen, the great American social critic, whose damning phrase "conspicuous consumption" sums up so much of the waste inherent in life's fast lanes. There should be more to life than that, he argued, and he knew where to find it.

"The country town is one of the great American institutions," Veblen wrote in 1923, "– perhaps the greatest, in the sense that it has had a greater part than any other in shaping public sentiment, and giving character to American culture."

ALBUQUERQUE, NEW MEXICO
A staple ingredient in southwest cuisine, freshly harvested
chili peppers hang out to dry in the sun.

NAVAJO ELDER, NEW MEXICO
Time and the elements have only added to the pride,
dignity and quiet determination of this elder's face.

FIDDLE CONTEST, SOUTH DAKOTA
When Roy and the boys go to it at an old-fashioned fiddle
contest, every foot in the place will be tapping.

HELENA, ARKANSAS
On the banks of the Mississippi, Helena hosts the annual
King Biscuit Blues Festival, one of the most popular
musical events in the South.

St. Paul, Minnesota

There's never a shortage of materials for the ice sculpture
contest during the Winter Carnival, but ladders are not
supplied.

SNOWMASS BALLOON FESTIVAL, COLORADO
Bright hot air balloons make this Aspen, Colorado,
festival one of the most colorful events around.

VERMONT
When the trees put on their best colors, a fresh coat of
paint seems only fitting.

THE WAIOLI HUIIA CHURCH, HAWAII
Ideally, the local place of worship should fit in with its
surroundings, and in Hawaii, green is the color of choice.

QUEEN FOR A DAY, WEST VIRGINIA
The float that everyone looks forward to – the reigning
beauty queen and her ladies-in-waiting.

Springfield, Illinois
Abraham Lincoln's hometown seems the suitable place for a historical military review.

OAHU, HAWAII
A hula show offers the pleasant distractions of sensual
dancing and tropical scenery. And no one could miss
seeing the band.

Strawberry Festival Concert, West Virginia
The high school band entertains proud parents and
passersby in the main square.

HOLLAND, MICHIGAN
(Opposite) Before the paint, the polish and the feet, a newly carved wooden shoe needs at least a week of drying in the open air.

FRESH FROM THE FIELD, TENNESSEE
Picking strawberries is back-breaking work, but the rewards all but compensate.

STATE FAIR, FLORIDA
Getting the pet pig ready for competition is usually a cooperative two-person operation. Deciding who holds the hose and who does the scrubbing usually isn't.

ANATONE, WASHINGTON
Evidently the mice, chicken and cows were absent on Census Day.

CAMDEN, MAINE
Double-parking, maritime style.

MYSTIC, CONNECTICUT
The Golden Age of Sail is vividly recalled at the Mystic
Seaport Museum, a faithful recreation of an early
nineteenth-century working New England coastal village.

CENTRAL TEXAS
A picnic takes on epic proportions when it comes to a
Texas chuckwagon cookout. Diets are best left at the door.

SWAMPSCOTT, MAINE
The deck shoes have replaced the boots at the Fireman's
Muster, but when it comes to manning the main hose, it's
still clenched teeth and grim determination.

MONTCLAIR, NEW JERSEY
Third-and-long, with an arboreal spectator dressed in its
best fall colors.

SANTE FE, NEW MEXICO
Taking a breather to show off the bargains found at the
annual Spanish Market.

SOUTH DAKOTA STATE FAIR
A summer tradition, and still the best place to take a date.

FIREWORKS, WEST VIRGINIA
A regatta's closing ceremonies compete in spectacle with
the Fourth of July.

CHURCH THEATER, GEORGIA
The parishioners of Big Bethel Church mount a
production of *Heaven Bound*.

OAKLAND, CALIFORNIA
Whether the market is in the city or in the country, the
produce still arrives before the sun.

NATCHEZ, MISSISSIPPI
No other city offers as large a collection of quintessential
Southern architecture as Natchez.

SUMMER HOMES, NORTH CAROLINA
It seems a constant battle to keep up with the Joneses
when it comes to gingerbread trim.

MAPLETOWN, IOWA

If you want an opinion on what to do about the problems of the nation, try the Main Street sidewalk cabinet meeting.

Photo Credits

Tom Algire/Tom Stack & Associates, 31, 45, 79

Craig Aurness/First Light Associated Photographers, 7, 8, 25, 27, 33, 35, 50, 55, 59, 67, 91, 93, 120

Cradoc Bagshaw/First Light Associated Photographers, 87

Annie Griffiths Belt/First Light Associated Photographers, 2-3, 56, 88, 97

Garry Briand/First Light Associated Photographers, 108

Mark Burnham/First Light Associated Photographers, 12

Charles Campbell/First Light Associated Photographers, 77, 98

Steve Chenn/First Light Associated Photographers, 30

Thomas Defeo/Virginia Division of Tourism, 76

Terry Donnelly/Tom Stack & Associates, 19

Janet Dwyer/First Light Associated Photographers, 15

Steve Elmore/Tom Stack & Associates, 86

David Fattaleh/Division of Tourism and Parks, State of West Virginia, 114

Georgia Department of Industry, Trade and Tourism, 39

A.C. Haralson/Arkansas Department of Parks & Tourism, 53, 95

Paul Horster/South Dakota Department of Tourism, 94

Illinois Department of Commerce and Community Affairs, 54, 101

Kenny Kemp/Division of Tourism and Parks, State of West Virginia, 103

Keith Kent/First Light Associated Photographers, 69

Larry Lee/First Light Associated Photographers, 118

John Luke/First Light Associated Photographers, 18

Wayne Lynch, 23, 36-37, 38, 60

Michael Philip Manheim/First Light Associated Photographers, 40, 48, 49, 61, 89, 96, 104, 109, 110

Peter McLeod/First Light Associated Photographers, 28, 57, 65

Michigan Travel Bureau, 78

Brian Milne/First Light Associated Photographers, 20-21, 85

Pat Morrow/First Light Associated Photographers, 71

Stig Nilsson/Florida Department of Commerce, Division of Tourism, 107

Mark Nohl/New Mexico Economic and Tourism Department, 68

North Carolina Division of Travel & Tourism, 90

Chuck O'Rear/First Light Associated Photographers, 13, 74

Rod Planck/Tom Stack & Associates, 46

Kenneth C. Poertner, 81, 106

Bob Pool/Tom Stack & Associates, 73

Peggy Powell/Division of Tourism and Parks, State of West Virginia, 100

Andrew Ptak/First Light Associated Photographers, 84

Michael S. Quinton, 47

Jim Richardson/First Light Associated Photographers, 1, 24, 44, 82, 83, 113, 116

Jeannine Rosenberg, 16

Bill Ross/First Light Associated Photographers, 10, 22, 32, 41

Kevin Schafer/Tom Stack & Associates, 117

Stephen Shaluta, Jr./Division of Tourism and Parks, State of West Virginia, 70

Stephen Sharnoff, 9, 66

Shattil/Rozinski/Tom Stack & Associates, 80

John Shaw/Tom Stack & Associates, 17

South Dakota Department of Tourism, 115

Mark Stephenson/First Light Associated Photographers, 5

J.D. Taylor, 42

Tennessee Tourist Development, 11, 29, 105

Texas Department of Commerce, 111

Travel Montana, 58

Greg Vaughn/Tom Stack & Associates, 51

Ron Watts/First Light Associated Photographers, 4, 52, 99, 102

D. Wilder/Tom Stack & Associates, 43

Doug Wilson/First Light Associated Photographers, 14

Dudley Witney, 6, 26, 34, 62, 63, 64, 72, 75, 119

Mike Yamashita/First Light Associated Photographers, 112

Jim Zuckerman/First Light Associated Photographers, 92